Paul Revere
Hero on Horseback

by Carol Domblewski

 HOUGHTON MIFFLIN HARCOURT
School Publishers

PHOTOGRAPHY CREDITS: **Cover** © Geoffrey Clements/CORBIS. **Title Page** © Bettmann/CORBIS. **2** © Bettmann/CORBIS. **3** © Bettmann/CORBIS. **4** The Granger Collection, New York. **5** Library of Congress, LC-DIG-ppmsca-01657. **6** © Bettmann/CORBIS. **9** © SuperStock, Inc. **12** © Geoffrey Clements/CORBIS. **13** © North Wind Picture Archives.

Printed in China

ISBN-13: 978-0-547-02649-7
ISBN-10: 0-547-02649-8

4 5 6 7 8 0940 18 17 16 15 14 13 12 11 10

Trouble was in the air in Boston in the spring of 1775. Bad feelings between the British and the colonists had been building up for years.

One problem was taxes. The British had won the French and Indian War in 1763. But the war had cost a lot of money. The British thought the colonists should help pay for it. So, the British started taxing the colonists. First, they passed the Stamp Act in 1765. Then they passed the Townshend Acts. These laws made the colonists pay for things they had never paid for before, such as tea and paper. The colonists thought these laws were unfair. Many were angry about it.

The colonists had to pay for and put stamps like these on all their newspapers and important papers.

Some people wanted to take action to stop the new laws. They were the Patriots. But it was not safe to be a Patriot. A Patriot at the time was someone who was working against the government. Then, as now, that was a serious crime. Then, as now, the government called that treason.

Paul Revere was one of these Patriots. By day, he was a silversmith. In his shop, he did the tedious work of making silver tea sets and other things by hand. However, his secret job was revolution. With others, he made plans against the British.

Paul Revere made beautiful silver objects. He also worked against the British.

The Boston Massacre

One day in 1770, an angry mob gathered in Boston. They began mocking the British soldier who was standing guard. Then they threw stones and snowballs. They terrified the guard.

The frightened guard called more soldiers. They opened fire on the crowd. That day three colonists died, and several more were wounded. The colonists called the event the Boston Massacre.

By 1770, many British soldiers believed that they lived in an enemy land.

Many colonists hung this picture in their homes.

Paul Revere helped make a picture to show what happened. He was not trying to mimic, or reproduce, the event exactly as it happened. Instead, the picture was more like a lie.

In Revere's picture, the British soldiers look evil. They are all lined up in a row. They look as if they planned to kill the people. On the other hand, the crowd looks innocent. No one is throwing things. No one looks angry.

The picture was sent all over the colonies. It helped stir up hate for the British.

The Tea Act

Then in 1773 Britain passed the Tea Act. Its goal was to cut the colonists out of the tea trade. Some people would lose a lot of money.

The Tea Act was a summons, or call to action. A group of men held the Boston Tea Party. No one drank any tea at this party. Instead, they threw tons of British tea into Boston Harbor. What did the British do?

Because they were breaking the law, the Patriots disguised themselves as American Indians.

The British were very angry when they found out about the dumping of the tea. Their answer was to close the Boston Harbor. No ships could go in or out. They also put an end to most town meetings. For some, this seemed like the end of liberty. People could not meet to discuss local issues. What had become of their rights?

The British sent a stronger army to the colonies, too. They made the colonists take soldiers to live in their homes. People were being watched. They had to speak their true feelings in whispers or in private. Rights and freedoms were gone. The people paid taxes, but they lacked the rights of British citizens. Anger was building.

1763	French and Indian War
1765	Stamp Act
1767	Townshend Acts
1770	Boston Massacre
1773	Tea Act
	Boston Tea Party
1775	Paul Revere's Ride
	War Begins

Fighting Back

Anger was perhaps greatest among the Sons of Liberty. There were Sons of Liberty all over the colonies. They were Patriots who loved freedom and were willing to fight for it.

The Sons of Liberty were angry at Great Britain for taking away their rights. They began writing to each other and working as a group. They formed an efficient network. They planned ways to take a stand.

Paul Revere was one of the Sons of Liberty. He had helped to organize the Boston Tea Party. However, his greatest fame doesn't come from his role in the Boston Tea Party. It doesn't come from his picture of the Boston Massacre either. Instead, it comes from his work as a messenger. He often rode on horseback to bring news to and from the Patriots. He helped set up secret meetings. He carried warnings to Patriots in danger.

Paul Revere's Famous Ride

The most famous ride Paul Revere ever took was in April 1775. By then, many colonists hated the British. They were getting ready to fight. The British were angry with the colonists, too. They saw trouble coming. The British got ready to stop the colonists.

In April 1775, some colonists heard secret news. The British were planning to march to the nearby town of Concord. It was twenty miles away from Boston. On the way, the British planned to arrest Patriot leaders.

The Patriots were preparing to fight.

The British could travel to Concord by land or by sea. The Patriots needed to know which way they were coming. So Paul Revere arranged for a signal that would appear in the tower of a church in Boston. The signal was one or two lanterns. One lantern meant "by land." Two meant "by sea." Patriots were watching from across the river.

But Revere did more than arrange for a signal. He personally crossed the river to Charlestown. He did it in darkness so that no one would see him. During the night, two men took him across in a rowboat.

A British warship was docked in the Charles River. British sailors could have killed the men. Luckily, no one saw them. Still, the men rowed as quietly as they could. They even covered the ends of the oars to keep them from making any sound.

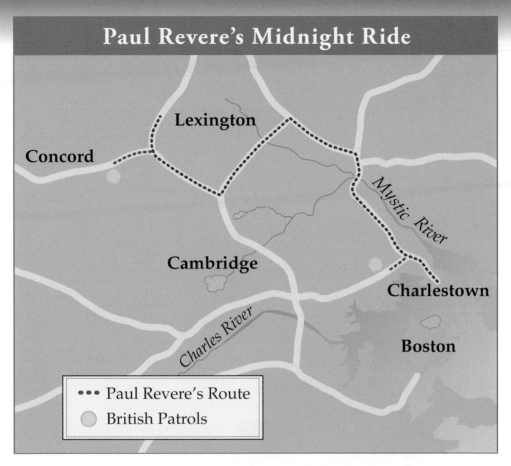

Paul Revere's Midnight Ride

Concord

Lexington

Cambridge

Mystic River

Charlestown

Charles River

Boston

••• Paul Revere's Route
⬤ British Patrols

If the signal was "by sea," then the British were coming across the Charles River by boat.

After the crossing, Revere crawled onto the shore. Some Patriots were waiting for him there. They had seen the signal. They had a horse ready for Revere. Now he could ride down the rural roads to warn others who had not seen the signal. He set off quickly for Lexington.

All along the way on that moonlit night, he passed the homes of colonists. At each place, he called out a warning. He yelled, "The Regulars are coming." People knew that meant that the British were coming.

The Patriots went into action. People grabbed their guns. All over the countryside, colonists got ready to fight. Soon, the peal of church bells rang out. The bells called more people to action.

Revere rode through the night.

The British had to run for their lives. Many never made it back to Boston.

Revere rode fast and hard. At one point, British soldiers saw him and chased him, but he lost them. He made it to Lexington. His most important job was to warn two leaders there, John Hancock and Sam Adams. The British wanted to capture them. That would surely mean they would be shipped to England to hang. Revere got there in time, and the men escaped.

Then Revere set off for Concord. On his way, he met more British soldiers. They held him for a while and took his horse. But his work was done. Because they had been warned, the Patriots were ready for the British.

Index

Responding

TARGET VOCABULARY **Word Builder** The words *peal* and *peel* are homophones. They sound alike but have different spellings and different meanings. Write the homophone for each of these words: *flour, one, made, through.*

Word	Homophone
bored	board

Write About It

Text to Text The bells did not peal when Paul Revere rode. It was quiet. Describe the night when Paul Revere rode and warned the sleeping colonists. Use some of the words from your chart in your paragraph.

efficient	peal
lacked	personally
mimic	rural
mocking	summons
organize	tedious

TARGET STRATEGY **Monitor/Clarify** Notice what is confusing as you read. Find ways to understand it.

Word Teaser Which vocabulary word rhymes with a word that describes a full suitcase?